Baby Farm Animals

Baby Llamas

By Nick Rebman

level 1 little blue readers

www.littlebluehousebooks.com

Little Blue House is distributed by North Star Editions:
sales@northstareditions.com | 888-417-0195

Produced for Little Blue House by Red Line Editorial.

Photographs ©: Shutterstock Images, cover, 4, 7, 9, 11, 12, 15, 17, 18, 20–21, 23, 24 (top left), 24 (top right), 24 (bottom left), 24 (bottom right)

Library of Congress Control Number: 2021916788

ISBN
978-1-64619-477-3 (hardcover)
978-1-64619-504-6 (paperback)
978-1-64619-557-2 (ebook pdf)
978-1-64619-531-2 (hosted ebook)

Printed in the United States of America
Mankato, MN
012022

About the Author

Nick Rebman is a writer and editor who lives in Minnesota. He enjoys reading, drawing, and taking long walks with his dog.

Table of Contents

mother

Baby Llamas

A baby llama is born.

Its mother stays near.

The baby llama
stands up.
Soon it can walk.

The baby llama walks
in a field.
It stands near a plant.

plant

The baby llama has
big ears.
It also has a long neck.

ear
neck

Eating and Drinking

The baby llama needs food.

It gets milk from its mother.

Soon the baby llama starts to eat grass. It eats other plants, too.

grass

The baby llama needs to drink. It gets water from a stream.

stream

Growing Up

The baby llama rests
on the grass.
It sleeps outside.

The baby llama lives
in a group.
The group is called
a herd.

The baby llama starts to grow up.
Soon it will have its own babies.

Glossary

field

milk

grass

stream

Index